The Book of the Nephilim

By Enoch

Copyright © 2023 Lamp of Trismegistus. All rights reserved. No part of this publication may be reproduced or transmitted in any form or by any means, electronic or mechanical, including photocopying, recording, or by any information storage and retrieval system, without permission in writing from Lamp of Trismegistus. Reviewers may quote brief passages.

ISBN: 978-1-63118-627-1

Christian Apocrypha Series

Other Books in this Series and Related Titles

The Lost Book of Noah by Noah (978-1-63118-624-0)

The Book of Astronomical Secrets by Enoch (978-1-63118-443-7)

The Book of Parables by Enoch (978-1-63118-429-1)

Second Book of Enoch by Enoch (978-1-63118-617-2)

The Book of Wisdom of Solomon by King Solomon (978-1-63118-502-1)

Book of the Watchers by Enoch (978-1-63118-615-8)

The Apocalypse of Peter by Peter (978-1-63118-527-4)

The Acts of the Apostle John by John (978-1-63118-622-6)

The Gospel of the Nativity of Mary by St. Matthew (978-1-63118-448-2)

The Vision of Saint Paul the Apostle by Paul (978-1-63118-526-7)

Early Translation of the Acts of the Apostles by Luke (978-1-63118-521-2)

The Hymn of Jesus by G. R. S. Mead (978-1-63118-409-3)

Psalms of Solomon by King Solomon (978-1-63118-439-0)

The First and Second Gospels of the Infancy of Jesus Christ (978-1-63118-415-4)

The Testament of Abraham by Abraham (978-1-63118-441-3)

The Lives of Adam and Eve by Moses (978-1-63118-414-7)

The Acts of Saint Andrew by Andrew (978-1-63118-623-3)

Lost Chapters of the Book of Daniel and Related Writings (978-1-63118-417-8)

The Testament of Moses by Moses (978-1-63118-440-6)

Testaments of the Twelve Patriarchs (978-1-63118-579-3)

The Odes of Solomon by King Solomon (978-1-63118-503-8)

Audio Versions are also Available on Audible, Amazon and Apple

Other Books in this Series and Related Titles

The Hidden Mysteries of Christianity by Annie Besant (978–1–63118–534–2)

The Ascension of Isaiah by Isaiah (978-1-63118-620-2)

The Hymns of Hermes by G. R. S. Mead (978-1-63118-405-5)

Freemasonry and the Egyptian Mysteries by C. W. Leadbeater (978-1-63118-456-7)

The Sepher Yetzirah and the Qabalah by M P Hall (978-1-63118-481-9)

Book of Dreams by Enoch (978-1-63118-437-6)

The Historic, Mythic and Mystic Christ by Annie Besant (978–1–63118–533–5)

The Fourth-Gospel and Synoptical Problem by G R S Mead (978–1–63118–576–2)

Masonic Symbolism of King Solomon's Temple by A Mackey &c (978-1-63118-442-0)

The Crest-Jewel of Wisdom by Adi Shankara (978-1-63118-475-8)

Kali the Mother by Sister Nivedita (978-1-63118-558-8)

The Brotherhood of Religions by Annie Besant (978–1–63118–563–2)

What Theosophy Does for Us by C W Leadbeater (978–1–63118–574–8)

Buddhist Psalms by Shinran (978-1-63118-465-9)

Catholicism, Yoga and Hinduism by Hartmann &c (978-1-63118-478-9)

Masonic Symbolism of Easter and the Christ in Masonry (978-1-63118-434-5)

Tao Te Ching & Commentary by Lao Tzu & C Johnston (978-1-63118-495-6)

Ancient Mysteries and Secret Societies by M P Hall (978-1-63118-410-9)

The Golden Verses of Pythagoras: Five Translations (978-1-63118-479-6)

Freemasonry & Catholicism by Max Heindel (978-1-63118-508-3)

A Few Masonic Sermons by A. C. Ward &c (978-1-63118-435-2)

Audio versions are also available on Audible, Amazon and Apple

Table of Contents

Series Introduction...8
Introduction...9

The Book of the Nephilim

I: *Enoch as a Just Man*...13
II: *Parable of Enoch on the Future Lot of the Wicked and the Righteous*...15
III: *Vision of the Holy One in the Heavens*...17
IV: *Prophecy for a Future Generation*...19
V: *The Fall of the Watchers*...21
VI: *The Watchers and the Nephilim*...23
VII: *200 Fallen Angels Led by Semjâzâ*...25
VIII: *Descending on Mount Hermon*...27
IX: *Swearing an Oath to Take Human Wives*...29
X: *Creation of the Nephilim*...31
XI: *Giants Born from the Union of Angels and Humans*...33
XII: *Consumption of Human Resources*...35
XIII: *Devouring Mankind and Other Living Beings*...37
XIV: *Azâzêl's Teachings*...39
XV: *Weapon Making*...41
XVI: *Metalworking*...42
XVII: *Beautification and Adornments*...43
XVIII: *Other Teachings*...45
XIX: *Enchantments*...47
XX: *Astrology*...49
XXI: *Knowledge of Clouds, Earth, Sun, and Moon*...51
XXII: *The Appeal of the Archangels*...53
XXIII: *Michael, Uriel, Raphael, and Gabriel Appeal to God*...55
XXIV: *Uriel's Mission to Warn Noah of the Coming Cataclysm*...57
XXV: *Punishment of the Fallen Angels*...59
XXVI: *Raphael Binds Azâzêl*...61

XXVII: *Imprisonment in Darkness*…63
XXVIII: *Final Judgment in the Fire*…65
XXIX: *Gabriel's Instructions Regarding the Nephilim*…66
XXX: *Destruction of the Nephilim*…67
XXXI: *Imprisonment of the Fallen Angels*…69
XXXII: *Michael Binds Semjâzâ and Associates*…71
XXXIII: *Imprisonment for Seventy Generations*…73
XXXIV: *Confinement in the Abyss of Fire*…75
XXXV: *The Judgment and Consummation of the Fallen Angels*…77
XXXVI: *The Eternal Binding of the Condemned*…79

SERIES INTRODUCTION

The Apocrypha are a loosely knit series of books, written by early vanguards of Christianity (covering the eras of both the old and new testaments), and which comprise somewhere between about a dozen to several hundred titles, depending on whom you ask and how that person defines "Apocrypha." A small selection of these can still be found included in the Catholic bible, while a majority of the books in question, were abandoned by church officials in the early centuries of Christianity. Many of these apocryphal books were originally considered canon by early followers of Christ, in the first four centuries following his birth. It wasn't until the meeting of the Council of Nicaea in 325, that Emperor Constantine and a group of roughly 300 church bishops, gathered together with the goal of defining, standardizing and unifying an otherwise splintering Christianity, that many of these writings ceased to be included in the newly established canon. Enjoy then, this book as an example, of just one of the many books of the Christian Apocrypha, and be sure to check out other titles in this series.

INTRODUCTION

The Nephilim:
An Analysis of Their Origins and the Importance of Enoch

The Nephilim, often translated as "the fallen ones" or "giants," are a group of beings referenced in ancient Jewish texts, primarily in the Book of Genesis of the Old Testament and the Book of Enoch, a non-canonical Jewish apocryphal work. The Nephilim are depicted as the offspring of heavenly beings known as the "Watchers" and human women, which ultimately leads to a divine cataclysm. Enoch, a biblical figure and the author of the Book of Enoch, plays a significant role in the narrative and understanding of the Nephilim.

The Nephilim and Their Origins

Genesis 6:1-4 offers an intriguing, albeit brief, introduction to the Nephilim. Here, they are the offspring of the "sons of God" and the "daughters of men," an odd coupling that has spurred centuries of theological debate. They are described as "mighty men of old, men of renown," suggesting an imposing presence and notable influence during their time. However, these verses provide little in the way of specific detail, leaving the identity of the "sons of God" and the nature of the Nephilim largely shrouded in mystery.

The Book of Enoch, a Jewish apocryphal work attributed to Enoch, the great-grandfather of Noah, provides a more detailed account of the origins of the Nephilim. This text expands upon the cryptic references in Genesis, offering a narrative that is both fascinating and unsettling.

Within this narrative, the "sons of God" are identified as the Watchers, a class of celestial beings known for their vigilance and wisdom. They are heavenly in origin, but their curiosity and desire lead them astray. Approximately two hundred Watchers, captained by a prominent figure named Semjâzâ, forsake their heavenly abode and descend onto Mount

Hermon. This descent is not merely a physical one; it symbolizes their fall from divine grace.

Upon their arrival on Earth, the Watchers become enamored with human women. Despite understanding the gravity of their actions and the potential divine repercussions, they cannot resist their earthly desires. They swear a mutual oath, promising to stand by their decision to intermingle with humanity. This pact reveals their defiance, their shared resolve in the face of potential divine wrath.

The unions between the Watchers and human women result in the birth of the Nephilim, a term often translated as "fallen ones" or "giants." These creatures are hybrids, part celestial and part human, embodying a dangerous fusion of the earthly and the divine. They are gigantic in stature, their size reflective of their extraordinary origin.

Yet, their existence is marked by strife and destruction. They consume vast amounts of resources, pushing humanity to the brink of ruin. They are insatiable, their appetites as enormous as their bodies. Their presence disrupts the natural order, leading to chaos and widespread suffering.

Their behavior echoes the transgressions of their celestial fathers, emphasizing the destructive consequences of crossing divine boundaries. Just as the Watchers overstepped their celestial limits, the Nephilim overstep earthly ones. Their existence, born from a breach of the divine order, ultimately results in a world teetering on the brink of annihilation. In this sense, the Nephilim are more than just creatures of myth and legend; they represent a dire warning about the dangers of transgressing the laws of the divine order.

Enoch's Importance to the Nephilim

Enoch stands as a pivotal figure in understanding the Nephilim's origins and their eventual demise. The Book of Enoch serves as one of the primary sources for their detailed narrative, beyond what is mentioned in Genesis. This text positions Enoch as a mediator between heaven and earth, and specifically, between God and the Watchers.

Firstly, Enoch's importance is underscored by his righteousness and piety, which sets him apart from other mortals. He is chosen to deliver God's judgment to the Watchers, pronouncing their punishment for corrupting humanity. In doing so, he embodies the role of a prophet, warning of the divine retribution that awaits the wicked while offering hope to the righteous.

Secondly, Enoch's role as a scribe further emphasizes his significance. He is tasked with recording the proceedings of the heavenly court, which includes the transgressions of the Watchers and the fate of their offspring, the Nephilim. This narrative, preserved here, becomes a historical and moral lesson for future generations.

Lastly, Enoch's ascent to heaven, where he is transformed into the angel Metatron, further highlights his importance. His transformation signifies divine approval and establishes him as an authoritative figure concerning heavenly matters. As Metatron, he continues to play a crucial role in managing the affairs of the heavenly realm, including those relating to the fallen angels and the Nephilim.

The Nephilim, as presented here and in the Book of Enoch, embody the disastrous consequences of a breach in the divine order, where celestial beings interfere with human affairs. The figure of Enoch, in his roles as a scribe, prophet, and angel, is pivotal to our understanding of these beings. He serves as a conduit for divine judgment, a chronicler of cosmic events, and a symbol of divine justice. The narrative of Enoch and the Nephilim continues to fascinate, serving as a stark reminder of the boundaries between the divine and the mortal, and the consequences of their transgression.

Chapter I:
Enoch as a Just Man

1. Enoch, the seventh of Adam's line, did stand as a testament to righteousness in an era of growing sin and iniquity. Amidst a realm descending into chaos, Enoch shone as a lighthouse of virtue, a stalwart of piety in a time when wickedness did multiply.

2. With the Lord did Enoch walk, a saying signifying his deep and abiding kinship with the Divine. In contrast to the many, Enoch held fast to his spiritual communion with God, marked by dutiful obedience, deep reverence, and a faith that faltered not.

3. His days bore witness to his godliness. He did not partake in the common wickedness, but chose the path of righteousness. The character of Enoch, untainted by the prevalent transgressions of his era, set him as a beacon amidst his brethren.

4. Enoch was also blessed with wisdom and understanding, as his teachings and writings do testify. With divine insights was he endowed, unraveling the mysteries of the heavens and the earth. His wisdom extended beyond the confines of earthly matters; he was privy to the celestial sphere, a bridge betwixt the divine and mortal realms.

5. His righteousness was acknowledged by the Almighty, who called Enoch unto Himself before his appointed time. This extraordinary culmination of his earthly journey bears further witness to his exceptional piety. Enoch tasted not the sting of death; he was taken, a testament to his intimate fellowship with God and his unwavering righteousness.

6. The tale of Enoch shines as a beacon of hope, proclaiming that righteousness and godliness are not overlooked by the Lord. His life serves as a blueprint for virtuous living, a guiding light for

generations to come. His wisdom and teachings echo through the ages, offering valuable counsel for those who seek to lead a life pleasing unto God.

7. As Noah's great-grandfather, the righteous lineage of Enoch played a crucial role in the preservation of mankind during the great deluge. His virtuous legacy lived on through his descendants, notably Noah, ensuring the perpetuation of humanity.

8. In the narrative of the Nephilim, the role of Enoch is of paramount importance. He presents a stark contrast to the fallen angels and their progeny. His steadfast adherence to God's laws and his righteous spirit stand in direct opposition to the rebellion and defilement brought forth by the Nephilim and their celestial fathers. Enoch, in his righteousness, embodies the potential for mankind's goodness, while the Nephilim, in their ruinous path, represent the dire consequences of defying the divine order.

Chapter II:
Parable of Enoch on the Future Lot of the Wicked and the Righteous

1. Enoch, filled with divine insight, proclaimed a parable before the sons of men, revealing the fate of the wicked and the righteous in the days to come.

2. "Hear, O children of earth, the words of Enoch your forefather, for the Holy One has granted me a vision of the future.

3. There shall come a time when the wicked will reap the bitter harvest of their deeds. Their transgressions shall be like a heavy yoke upon their shoulders, and they will find no peace.

4. The wicked, who have chosen the path of corruption, who have slandered the righteous and shunned the commandments of the Holy One, will face a great reckoning.

5. The Holy One, the Judge of all, will cast them into the abyss, where there will be weeping and gnashing of teeth. Their cries will rise up, but they will find no mercy, for they showed none.

6. The souls of the wicked will yearn for relief, but they shall find none. The torment of their punishment will be as unending as their sins were countless.

7. But fear not, children of righteousness, for your lot is vastly different. The Holy One has seen your deeds and marked your faithfulness.

8. The righteous, who have walked in the path of the Holy One, who have loved their neighbors and upheld justice, will receive the reward of their virtue.

9. The Holy One will lead them to His holy mountain, where they will bask in His glorious light, and their joy will be unending.

10. They will dwell in peace, untouched by the torment that befalls the wicked. Their path will be straight, and their steps will not falter.

11. The righteous will shine like the stars in the heavens, and they will sing the praises of the Holy One. They will dwell in His presence, and their happiness will never cease.

12. This, then, is the future lot of the wicked and the righteous. Heed my words, children of the earth, for the time of judgment is at hand."

13. With these words, Enoch closed his parable, leaving the sons of men to ponder the weight of his prophecy and the choice that lay before them: the path of wickedness leading to torment, or the path of righteousness leading to eternal joy.

Chapter III:
Vision of the Holy One in the Heavens

1. Enoch, a just man, was granted a divine vision by the Lord, and his eyes were opened to behold the Holy One in the heavens.

2. The sons of God revealed to Enoch the mysteries of the celestial realms, and from their teachings, Enoch gained knowledge of all that he saw.

3. The vision was not for Enoch's generation, but for a future generation that had yet to come, and in that time, the message would be revealed.

4. Enoch beheld the glory of the Holy One, surrounded by a multitude of angels, and he was struck with awe and reverence.

5. The voice of the Holy One spoke to Enoch, revealing to him the secrets of creation, the movements of the celestial bodies, and the eternal cycle of life and death.

6. Enoch was shown the heavenly throne, where the Holy One ruled with justice and mercy over all the inhabitants of the earth and the heavens.

7. The archangels, Michael, Uriel, Raphael, and Gabriel, stood by the side of the Holy One, ready to carry out His divine commands.

8. In his vision, Enoch saw the fall of the Watchers, the angels who took human wives, and he understood the consequences of their transgressions upon the earth.

9. The Holy One revealed to Enoch the coming judgment upon the fallen angels and the Nephilim, and the cleansing of the earth through a great deluge.

10. Enoch was shown the future generations of the righteous, who would live in peace and harmony under the guidance of the Messiah.

11. The Holy One commanded Enoch to write down all that he had seen and learned, and to share this knowledge with the future generations, so they might be prepared for the coming trials and the ultimate redemption.

12. With his vision complete, Enoch returned to the earth, forever changed by the divine knowledge he had received, and committed his life to sharing the wisdom of the Holy One with all who would listen.

Chapter IV:
Prophecy for a Future Generation

1. Enoch, having completed his parable, then turned his gaze to a distant future, speaking prophecy for a generation yet unborn.

2. "Hear me, O future children of earth," began Enoch, "For the Holy One has shown me what is to come, a time far beyond my own.

3. You shall exist in a world transformed, where the deeds of your ancestors will echo in the wind, their triumphs and failings shaping your path.

4. But heed this prophecy, children of the future, for it is a warning and a promise from the Holy One Himself.

5. There will come a time when the earth will shudder and groan under the weight of wickedness. Corruption will spread like a blight, and the cries of the oppressed will reach the heavens.

6. But despair not, for in these darkest hours, the Holy One will not abandon His creation. He will remember the covenant He made with your forefathers, and He will act.

7. A chosen one will rise among you, a beacon of righteousness in the shadow of wickedness. He will carry the light of the Holy One, and His words will be a balm to the afflicted.

8. His path will be arduous, and he will face great tribulations. But he will stand firm, for the Holy One will be his strength and his shield.

9. Through him, the Holy One will bring justice to the oppressed, and the wicked will face their reckoning. The blight of corruption will be cleansed, and the earth will breathe anew.

10. In that time, the righteous will rejoice, for their prayers will have been answered. Their joy will be like a river, their praises like a mighty chorus.

11. So, future children of earth, remember this prophecy. Remember the promises of the Holy One, and hold fast to the path of righteousness. For in doing so, you will ensure the survival of your world and the triumph of justice over wickedness."

12. And with that, Enoch ceased speaking, leaving his prophecy to echo through the ages, a message of hope and a call to righteousness for the generations yet to come.

Chapter V:
The Fall of the Watchers

1. Enoch then began to speak of the time when the Watchers, the angels of the highest heavens, abandoned their celestial dwellings to descend upon the earth.

2. "Led by their chieftain, Sêmîazâz," he said, "two hundred of the Watchers descended upon the summit of Mount Hermon."

3. "They swore an oath upon the mountain, binding themselves to their plan, despite the great sin they were about to commit."

4. The Watchers, filled with lust for human women, took them as wives, an act against the divine order.

5. "These unions," Enoch recounted, "gave birth to a race of giants, the Nephilim, whose height reached three hundred ells."

6. The Nephilim, the offspring of the Watchers and human women, consumed the resources of men and when they could no longer be sustained, turned against humankind.

7. They began to sin against the other creatures of the earth, devouring birds, beasts, reptiles, and fish, and consuming one another's flesh.

8. The fallen Watchers, not content with their perversion of natural order, began to teach mankind forbidden knowledge.

9. Azâzêl, one of the leaders of the Watchers, taught men how to make weapons and to work the metals of the earth. He showed them how to make jewelry and use cosmetics, introducing vanity and warfare into the hearts of men.

10. Semjâzâ, another leader, taught enchantments and root-cuttings, leading mankind further astray from the path of righteousness.

11. The Watchers, in their rebellion, had corrupted the earth and its inhabitants, leading them away from the peace and simplicity intended by the Holy One.

12. Observing this corruption, the archangels Michael, Uriel, Raphael, and Gabriel appealed to the Holy One to pass judgement on the fallen Watchers and the earth.

13. The Holy One, hearing their pleas, sent Uriel to warn Noah of the coming flood, which would cleanse the earth of its corruption.

14. Raphael was commanded to bind Azâzêl and cast him into the darkness as punishment for his sins against the Holy One and the earth.

15. The Holy One also commanded Gabriel to deal with the Nephilim, the offspring of the fallen Watchers and human women.

16. Michael, the chief of the archangels, was ordered to bind the remaining fallen Watchers, and seal them away until the day of their final judgement.

17. Thus, Enoch recounted, the fall of the Watchers was a tale of rebellion and corruption, but also of divine justice and the hope for redemption.

Chapter VI:
The Watchers and the Nephilim

1. Enoch recounted the tale of the Watchers, a divine assembly of celestial beings who were assigned to watch over the earth and its inhabitants.

2. "In the days of Jared," Enoch said, "two hundred Watchers, led by their chieftain Sêmîazâz, descended on the summit of Mount Hermon."

3. "They swore a mutual oath, binding themselves to their plan, and took human women as wives, in defiance of divine law."

4. From these forbidden unions, the Nephilim were born, a race of giants towering three hundred ells high, whose strength and stature surpassed all creatures on the earth.

5. "These Nephilim," Enoch continued, "were not of the natural world, but a product of the Watchers' transgression."

6. As the Nephilim grew, they consumed the resources of mankind. When these proved insufficient, they turned against man and beast, sinning against the natural order of the world.

7. The Nephilim plagued the earth with violence and chaos, terrorizing humanity and causing widespread suffering.

8. Meanwhile, the Watchers watched over their progeny, their hearts filled with a forbidden love for their offspring.

9. Despite the chaos they had unleashed upon the world, the Watchers did not repent. Instead, they further indulged in their transgressions, teaching mankind forbidden knowledge.

10. Azâzêl, one of the leaders of the Watchers, showed men how to forge weapons and adorn themselves with precious stones and cosmetics, thus introducing warfare and vanity into the world.

11. Semjâzâ, another leader, taught enchantments and root-cuttings, driving mankind further from righteousness.

12. Thus, the Watchers and their progeny, the Nephilim, brought ruin upon the earth, leading mankind astray from the divine path and toward a future of corruption and violence.

Chapter VII:
200 Fallen Angels Led by Semjâzâ

1. In the time of Jared, as Enoch recounted, a group of two hundred angels descended from the heavens.

2. These celestial beings, known as the Watchers, were led by a powerful entity named Semjâzâ.

3. Semjâzâ, their leader, was a being of formidable presence and authority, and his voice commanded obedience among the celestial host.

4. Upon the summit of Mount Hermon, Semjâzâ gathered the Watchers, uniting them under his leadership.

5. Under the vast expanse of the celestial dome, Semjâzâ voiced his fears to his brethren, expressing uncertainty about the course of action they were contemplating.

6. "I fear," he confessed, "that you will not agree to this deed, and I alone shall bear the weight of this great sin."

7. However, his brethren, steadfast in their resolve, assured him of their commitment to their plan.

8. "Let us all swear an oath," they declared, "and bind ourselves by mutual imprecations not to abandon this plan but to carry out this deed."

9. And so, they all swore together, their voices echoing through the divine realm, binding themselves by mutual imprecations upon the summit of Mount Hermon.

10. From that moment, the place was known as Mount Hermon, a testament to their pact – for 'Hermon' means 'oath' or 'curse'.

11. Thus, united in purpose and bound by a solemn oath, these two hundred Watchers, led by Semjâzâ, set forth on their path of defiance against divine law.

Chapter VIII:
Descending on Mount Hermon

1. The Watchers descended from the heavens, their radiant forms piercing the veil of the firmament, and they came upon the summit of Mount Hermon.

2. The mountain trembled under their celestial weight, its lofty peak reaching up towards the heavens, but dwarfed by their divine stature.

3. Their heavenly light was cast upon the earth, a spectacle of celestial splendor, causing all living beings to shudder and gaze in wonder.

4. Upon Mount Hermon, these divine beings made their solemn oath, binding themselves to their chosen path, a path that deviated from the divine order of things.

5. Bound by their oath, they took a collective stand, affirming their commitment to their plan and to each other.

6. As each angel swore their oath, their voices resounded through the heavens and the earth, a chorus of divine defiance that echoed through the cosmos.

7. They named the mountain Hermon, a constant reminder of their irrevocable oath and the course of action they had chosen.

8. Their descent on Mount Hermon marked the beginning of a series of events that would have a profound impact on the earth and its inhabitants, and bring about repercussions felt across the heavenly and earthly realms.

9. From the height of Mount Hermon, the Watchers beheld the world of men, their gaze reaching into every corner of the earth.

10. With their descent, the balance between the celestial and earthly realms was upset, setting in motion a chain of events that would bring about an era of strife, turmoil, and upheaval.

Chapter IX:
Swearing an Oath to Take Human Wives

1. Among the fallen angels, their leader, Semjâzâ, spoke with a voice that thundered like the heavens, urging them to take human wives.

2. He voiced his fear, his celestial countenance displaying an emotion uncommon to divine beings, "I fear you may not agree to this deed, and I alone shall bear the burden of a great sin."

3. But the other angels, bound by their oath and driven by their shared desire, responded in unison, "Let us swear an oath, bind ourselves by mutual imprecations not to abandon this plan, but to do this thing."

4. Their voices resonated through the celestial ether, their words forming a pact that sealed their fates and the fates of those they would come to interact with.

5. So, they swore together, each angel adding their voice to the collective affirmation, reinforcing the bond that linked them.

6. Their mutual imprecations creating a pact, a bond stronger than the hardest diamond, unbreakable and resolute.

7. Their decision was made, and their course set, they would descend further, into the realm of men, and take human wives.

8. This oath, made upon the summit of Mount Hermon, echoed through the heavens, a testament to their intent and the beginning of a new era.

9. Their decision, irrevocable and resolute, marked the first step towards a path of interaction and interference with the world of men, a path that would have far-reaching implications.

10. The oath they made that day, on Mount Hermon, became a testament to their resolve and a prophecy of the upheavals that would follow.

Chapter X:
Creation of the Nephilim

1. As the fallen angels descended and mingled with mankind, the earth began to change, and the birth of the Nephilim marked a new era.

2. The angelic beings took human wives, and these unions bore fruit in the form of mighty beings, the Nephilim, who stood taller and stronger than any man.

3. The Nephilim, whose height reached three hundred ells, a size beyond human comprehension, roamed the earth, their presence a constant reminder of the unnatural union between angels and men.

4. The Nephilim, with their extraordinary strength and stature, consumed all the acquisitions of men, their insatiable appetites causing distress among mankind.

5. When men could no longer sustain them, the Nephilim turned against them, their hunger unsatisfied, they devoured mankind.

6. Not content with the destruction of humanity, they began to sin against the creatures of the earth, birds, and beasts, and reptiles, and fish, consuming their flesh and drinking their blood.

7. The Nephilim, the offspring of the fallen angels, became a blight upon the earth, their presence and actions disrupting the natural order of things, leading to chaos and suffering.

8. The world, under the influence of these beings, began to change, the natural laws bent and twisted, leading to an era of strife and conflict.

9. The creation of the Nephilim marked a turning point in the history of the earth, a time when the natural and supernatural intertwined, leading to consequences that would resonate throughout time.

Chapter XI:
Giants Born from the Union of Angels and Humans

1. In the days of old, when the divine yet fallen Watchers still roamed the Earth, their hearts turned towards the daughters of men, and from this forbidden union, a new progeny was conceived. These were the Giants, beings of immense stature and power, a fusion of the celestial and the terrestrial.

2. The conception of these Giants was unlike any other. The human women, blessed or cursed with this unusual offspring, bore children that grew rapidly, their size and might echoing the supernatural strength of their angelic fathers.

3. Towering over the tallest trees and dwarfing the highest of human-made structures, these Giants were an awe-inspiring sight. Their stature made them appear as moving mountains, their footsteps causing the ground to tremble beneath them.

4. The strength they wielded was not of this world, reflecting the might of their celestial parentage. They uprooted ancient trees as if they were saplings, moved boulders larger than houses as if they were mere pebbles. Their laughter was thunderous, their voices like the roaring of the sea.

5. Their unique heritage was evident in their features - their beauty was celestial, reflecting the visage of their angelic fathers, yet their bodies, solid and robust, bore the mark of their human mothers. This blend of the ethereal and the earthly gave them an uncanny, captivating appearance.

6. However, their colossal size and extraordinary power came with a price. The Giants consumed food and drink in quantities that far exceeded what the land and its people could provide. As their

hunger grew, they devoured all the acquisitions of men, leaving famine and despair in their wake.

7. The presence of these Giants, the offspring of the Watchers and human women, cast a shadow over the world. Their existence was a stark and constant reminder of the unnatural union between the celestial and the earthly, a testament to the audacious overreach of the fallen angels.

8. Their presence incited a mixture of fear and awe among humans. These Giants were the living symbols of the heavenly transgression, the tangible evidence of the breaking of divine law.

9. Ultimately, the Giants, borne of the union between angels and human women, stood as a cautionary monument to the consequences of breaching divine boundaries. Their existence served as a constant reminder of the catastrophic effects of the Watchers' defiance of heavenly order.

Chapter XII:
Consumption of Human Resources

1. The mighty Giants, children of the celestial Watchers and earthly women, began to consume the resources of the world. They devoured the fruits of the land and the beasts of the field, their insatiable hunger leaving barren fields and empty pastures in its wake.

2. The once fertile valleys, teeming with wheat and barley, were left desolate. The Giants, with their supernatural strength, could pluck a tree from the ground as easily as a child picks a flower, leaving once lush forests stripped bare.

3. With their colossal size came a hunger that was never satisfied. They consumed livestock in droves, leaving farmers and shepherds in despair. Herds of cattle that once grazed on green pastures were reduced to mere bones and hide.

4. Their thirst was as boundless as their hunger. They drained rivers and lakes dry, leaving fish to die on the exposed riverbeds. The once vibrant life that teemed in these waters was replaced by death and desolation.

5. As the resources of the land dwindled, the Giants turned their attention to the seas. They drained the oceans of their fish, leaving the seabed exposed and the water lifeless.

6. The relentless consumption by the Giants brought about an era of scarcity and hardship for humans. Food became scarce, and water even more so. The bountiful Earth was being slowly devoured, inch by inch, by these celestial progeny.

7. The cries of despair from the humans reached the heavens. They pleaded for respite, for an end to the relentless consumption by

the Giants. But the Giants, in their insatiable hunger, paid no heed to the plight of humans.

8. The Giants' consumption of the Earth's resources was not merely a result of their physical needs. It was a display of power, a demonstration of their dominance over the Earth and its creatures.

9. As the land grew barren and the seas emptied, the world stood on the brink of ruin. The creation of the Giants, the result of the unholy union between the Watchers and humans, threatened to consume the world, leaving nothing but desolation in its wake.

Chapter XIII:
Devouring Mankind and Other Living Beings

1. When human sustenance could no longer satiate their ravenous appetites, the Giants turned their monstrous gaze upon mankind itself. Driven by a hunger beyond understanding, they began to feast upon human flesh, spreading terror and despair.

2. The Giants, massive in stature and terrible in their wrath, stalked through cities and villages alike, snatching up men, women, and children, consuming them without remorse or hesitation.

3. Their cruel laughter echoed through the valleys as they hunted their terrified victims, the sweet taste of human flesh only fueling their monstrous appetites. The giants reveled in their terror, the cries of their victims a macabre symphony to their ears.

4. But mankind was not the only victim of their insatiable hunger. They began to sin against the birds of the sky, the beasts of the field, and the fish of the sea, gorging themselves on their flesh.

5. They devoured birds by the flock, their great hands plucking them from the sky as easily as one might pick an apple from a tree. They consumed beasts with a single bite, their massive teeth tearing through fur and bone as if they were paper.

6. They drained the seas of their life, their giant forms wading through the waters and feasting on the countless fish within. The seas, once teeming with life, became a desolate wasteland, a testament to the Giants' insatiable hunger.

7. The Giants' horrific banquet did not stop with the consumption of flesh. They developed a vile thirst for the lifeblood of their victims. They drank greedily from their fallen prey, the life-giving liquid staining their lips a dark, ominous red.

8. The once prosperous land was now stained with blood and littered with bones. The Giants, born of the unholy union of Watchers and human women, had brought about an age of terror and despair, their monstrous appetites threatening to consume all life on Earth.

Chapter XIV:
Azâzêl's Teachings

1. The fallen angels, led by Azâzêl, sought not only to corrupt mankind through their offspring, the Giants, but also by imparting forbidden knowledge.

2. From the heavens they had descended, bringing with them the secrets of the celestial realm, knowledge that was forbidden to mankind.

3. Azâzêl, a Watcher of significant influence, took it upon himself to share forbidden knowledge with mankind, marking the beginning of their descent into sin.

4. He taught them the art of war, a concept foreign and dangerous to the peaceful beings they were meant to be. He unveiled the secrets of metalworking, showing them how to craft sharp swords, resilient shields, and piercing knives from the metals of the earth.

5. As if the knowledge of warfare was not destructive enough, Azâzêl also taught them to mine the earth for metals and precious stones, fostering avarice and strife over wealth and possessions.

6. He introduced them to the art of crafting these precious materials into ornaments, fostering vanity and pride among men and women, further distancing them from their original nature of simplicity and contentment.

7. Azâzêl's most insidious teaching was perhaps the use of antimony, the art of enhancing beauty with cosmetics. This led to a fixation on physical appearance, stirring lust, envy, and shallow judgments based on outward appearances.

8. The influence of Azâzêl's teachings was profound and devastating. It led to an era of godlessness, as mankind became consumed with their newfound power and beauty, forgetting the divine wisdom and guidance they were meant to follow.

Chapter XV:
Weapon Making

1. Azâzêl, in his teachings, first revealed to mankind the secrets of weapon-making, a knowledge that was meant to be hidden from them.

2. He showed them how to extract the metals from the earth, a process they had not known before. This involved mining and refining, skills that took humanity away from their peaceful existence and closer to destruction.

3. He then demonstrated how these metals could be shaped and sharpened into lethal weapons. He taught them to forge iron into swords and to mold bronze into shields, introducing warfare into human society.

4. The creation of knives followed, versatile tools that could be used for both peaceful and violent purposes. These weapons, though smaller, brought with them an increased potential for clandestine harm and personal violence.

5. With the knowledge imparted by Azâzêl, humans were no longer dependent on their environment for survival. They had the means to defend themselves, but also the power to attack, conquer, and kill. This was a turning point that marked the beginning of a violent era for mankind.

Chapter XVI:
Metalworking

1. Following the introduction of weaponry, Azâzêl further delved into the mysteries of metalworking. He opened the eyes of humanity to the potential of the earth's hidden treasures.

2. He showed them how to recognize and extract various types of metal ores. These included iron, copper, silver, and gold, each with its unique properties and value.

3. Azâzêl then demonstrated the complex process of refining these ores to obtain pure metals. He taught them about smelting, where they used high heat to separate the metal from the surrounding rock, a process that required skill and precision.

4. Once the metals were purified, Azâzêl revealed the secrets of molding and shaping them. He demonstrated how to make breastplates, providing humans with the knowledge to create their own armor for warfare.

5. He further taught them the art of creating ornamental pieces such as bracelets and other adornments. He showed them how to embed precious stones into these pieces, leading to the birth of jewelry-making.

6. This knowledge, while providing humans with new abilities and creativity, also instilled in them a new form of greed. The pursuit of these metals and the wealth they represented would become a source of strife and conflict among humanity.

Chapter XVII:
Beautification and Adornments

1. Azâzêl, the fallen angel, endowed humanity with knowledge far beyond their understanding. In the realm of aesthetics, he introduced the idea of physical adornment, completely transforming the simple lives humans led until then.

2. He taught them the use of antimony, a brittle, silvery-white metallic element. This marked the birth of cosmetics, as humans began to apply this knowledge to enhance their appearance, focusing especially on the eyes.

3. With the use of ground antimony, he showed the people how to darken their eyelids. This created a captivating allure as the eyes appeared larger and more profound, the window to the soul framed in a new and striking way.

4. The art of makeup, now a common practice, emerged from these teachings. Azâzêl's lessons were a turning point in human evolution, allowing self-expression through physical modification.

5. Not only did he introduce the use of antimony, but Azâzêl also brought forth knowledge of precious stones and gems. He taught the humans to cut, polish, and set these precious stones into the metal pieces they had learned to craft, leading to the creation of jewelry - a form of adornment still revered today.

6. His lessons didn't stop at natural beauty. Azâzêl taught humans to create various coloring tinctures from plants and minerals. These were used for body decoration, for dyeing fabrics, and for creating vibrant artwork. Fashion and personal expression through clothing thus found its roots in these teachings.

7. The knowledge Azâzêl imparted had far-reaching implications. It led to the birth of new industries and crafts, creating opportunities for trade and increasing the wealth and prosperity of societies.

8. However, the pursuit of beauty and the desire for adornment also brought forth negative consequences. It led to vanity and an obsession with physical appearance, drawing people away from spiritual pursuits and fostering materialism.

9. This obsession spurred social differentiation, as those who could afford more expensive adornments were considered superior. Envy, competition, and societal divisions grew, further fueling the moral decay that the fallen angels had initiated.

10. The teachings of Azâzêl, while contributing to the evolution of human society in significant ways, also played a part in its moral degradation. The pursuit of physical beauty and adornment, once non-existent, became a driving force in human interaction and societal structure.

Chapter XVIII:
Other Teachings

1. Beyond Azâzêl's teachings of weaponry, metalwork, and adornments, other fallen angels passed on their own forbidden knowledge. This knowledge was not meant for mortal beings, yet it found its way into their grasp, forever altering the course of human civilization.

2. Semjâzâ, another leader among the fallen angels, introduced the practices of enchantments and root-cuttings to humanity. He taught them how to harness the mystical energies of the world, to manipulate nature and command unseen forces. This knowledge created a dangerous imbalance, as humans, unprepared for such power, used it recklessly.

3. Armârôs, too, imparted his wisdom, showing humanity how to dissolve enchantments. He shared the secrets of counteracting the very energies Semjâzâ had taught them to command. This knowledge, while seemingly benign, led to an escalation in mystical power struggles, further corrupting society.

4. Barâqîjâl introduced astrology, revealing the secrets of the cosmos to humanity. He taught them to read the stars and planets, to interpret their movements and patterns. This knowledge, while enriching human understanding of the universe, also led to superstition and fatalism, as people began to attribute their fortunes and misfortunes to celestial events.

5. Kôkabêl shared his wisdom of the constellations, teaching humans to map the night sky. This knowledge aided navigation and marked the birth of astronomy, but it also furthered the obsession with celestial divination.

6. Ezêqêêl taught the knowledge of the clouds, enabling humans to predict weather patterns. This proved vital for agriculture, but also led to a heightened fear and reverence of natural disasters.

7. Araqiêl shared the signs of the earth, teaching humans to read the land for signs of water, minerals, and other resources. This improved survival, but also sparked greed and territorial disputes.

8. Shamsiêl conveyed the signs of the sun, teaching humans to measure time and seasons. This knowledge aided agriculture and planning but also created a heightened consciousness of mortality.

9. Sariêl revealed the course of the moon, laying the foundation for the lunar calendar. This enabled the tracking of tides and women's cycles, but also led to moon worship and associated rituals.

10. Each of these teachings contributed to the progression of human civilization, but they also brought about unforeseen complications. The knowledge meant for divine beings was now in the hands of humans, leading them down a path of both enlightenment and destruction.

Chapter XIX:
Enchantments

1. The fallen angel Semjâzâ took it upon himself to reveal to humanity the secrets of enchantments. This knowledge, previously exclusive to the divine, was shared with humans, transforming their understanding of the world around them.

2. Semjâzâ taught the humans to draw upon the latent spiritual energies that permeated the world. He showed them the intricate patterns and symbols that could channel this energy, directing it to specific purposes. They learned to create talismans and amulets, each etched with unique symbols to serve different purposes.

3. The power of protection was revealed to them, allowing humans to craft protective amulets that shielded them from harm. They also discovered how to create healing talismans, capable of mending injuries and curing diseases, enhancing their survival in a world fraught with danger.

4. But the teachings were not limited to benign applications. Semjâzâ also showed them how to craft weapons of spiritual power, how to curse and hex, and how to bind spirits into servitude. This knowledge provided them with formidable power, but also led them down a path of potential self-destruction.

5. The manipulation of the elements was another aspect of these teachings. The humans learned to call forth fire at will, to summon water from thin air, to mold the earth to their desires, and to command the winds. This ability to control the very elements bestowed them with a god-like power, altering the course of human development.

6. Semjâzâ also taught humans the power of words. He revealed to them that words were not just tools for communication, but they

could also be used to shape reality. Spells, incantations, and songs of power became part of their repertoire, adding a new layer of complexity to human interaction.

7. However, the newfound power was not always used wisely or justly. The knowledge of enchantments led to a rise in conflicts, as individuals used their powers to settle personal scores or to exert dominance over others. Communities were torn apart by magical feuds, leading to chaos and discord.

8. Thus, the teaching of enchantments, while opening up new possibilities for humanity, also led to unforeseen consequences. The balance of power was disrupted, and the very fabric of human society was irrevocably altered. The world was no longer the same, and humanity had to navigate through this new landscape, forever marked by the teachings of the fallen angel Semjâzâ.

Chapter XX:
Astrology

1. Barâqîjâl, another of the fallen angels, imparted the knowledge of astrology to humans. Before his teachings, the night sky was a mystery, a vast expanse dotted with twinkling lights. Afterward, it became a celestial map, filled with guidance, wisdom, and prophecy.

2. The humans were taught to understand the movements of the celestial bodies, how the positions of the stars, planets, and other celestial bodies had a profound influence on human life. This knowledge transformed their perception of the universe, making them aware of their place within a larger cosmic order.

3. Barâqîjâl showed them how to chart the heavens, to identify constellations and to track the path of planets. This knowledge enabled them to create the first astrological calendars, aligning their activities with the rhythms of the cosmos.

4. They were taught to read the celestial omens, to interpret the messages hidden in the dance of the stars. Celestial phenomena, like comets, eclipses, and meteor showers, were no longer seen as random occurrences, but as signs carrying divine messages.

5. The fallen angel taught them how to correlate the celestial patterns with events on Earth. They learned that the fluctuations in the celestial energy could influence human behavior, health, and fortune. This understanding gave birth to the practice of casting horoscopes, allowing them to foresee the potential future and guide their actions accordingly.

6. The teachings of Barâqîjâl also introduced a new dimension of spirituality to humans. They came to view the universe as a living entity, a grand cosmic orchestra playing the music of creation.

Their prayers, rituals, and ceremonies began to reflect this cosmic connection, aligning with celestial events like solstices, equinoxes, and planetary alignments.

7. However, this knowledge also carried the risk of misuse. Some began to use astrology to manipulate others, exploiting their fears and hopes for personal gain. The wisdom of the stars, meant to guide and enlighten, was sometimes twisted into a tool for control and deceit.

8. Despite the potential for misuse, the teachings of Barâqîjâl forever changed humanity's relationship with the cosmos. It ushered in a new era of understanding, a time when humans looked to the heavens for guidance, and found it in the patterns of the stars.

Chapter XXI:
Knowledge of Clouds, Earth, Sun, and Moon

1. Ezêqêêl, Araqiêl, Shamsiêl, and Sariêl, the remaining four fallen angels, imparted further knowledge to humans, each contributing their unique teaching to complete the breadth of wisdom the Watchers brought to Earth.

2. Ezêqêêl unfolded the mysteries of the clouds. He taught humans how to predict weather patterns and understand the signs of impending storms or fair weather. His teachings allowed mankind to better prepare for and adapt to changing weather, improving their ability to farm and navigate the seas.

3. Araqiêl, the second of these teachers, offered knowledge of the Earth. He taught humans to understand the nature of soil, rocks, and minerals. His teachings gave birth to early geology, agriculture, and mining, enabling humans to harness the resources of the Earth and advance their civilizations.

4. Shamsiêl, the third teacher, brought the wisdom of the Sun. He taught humans the nature of the Sun, its cycles, and its influence on the Earth. His teachings led to the creation of the solar calendar and an understanding of the seasons. It gave rise to early astronomy and the understanding of the Sun's vital role in supporting life.

5. Lastly, Sariêl imparted knowledge of the Moon. He revealed the phases of the Moon, its influence on the tides, and its role in marking the passage of time. The lunar calendar was born from his teachings, and with it, a deeper understanding of the cyclical nature of life.

6. Together, the teachings of these four fallen angels greatly expanded human knowledge and potential. However, like the

teachings of their brethren, these gifts were a double-edged sword. The knowledge allowed humans to thrive and advance, but it also opened up new avenues for corruption and misuse.

7. Some used their newfound understanding of the natural world to dominate others, exploiting resources and upsetting the delicate balance of nature. Yet, others used the wisdom to cultivate a deeper connection with the Earth and the cosmos, living in harmony with the natural world and using their knowledge for the betterment of all.

8. Thus, the legacy of the fallen angels' teachings is complex, reflecting both the light and shadow of human nature. It was a gift of knowledge that forever changed the trajectory of human history, for better or worse.

Chapter XXII:
The Appeal of the Archangels

1. As the Earth groaned under the weight of the giants and mankind suffered from the corruption and chaos the fallen angels brought, the Archangels Michael, Uriel, Raphael, and Gabriel watched with heavy hearts.

2. They saw the devastation and sorrow that had befallen the world, the beauty of God's creation marred by the sins of the Watchers and their offspring.

3. Unable to bear the sight of such desolation, they came together in a solemn conclave. Each spoke of the atrocities they had witnessed, their voices echoing with grief and anger.

4. Michael, the leader of the heavenly host, was the first to speak. He lamented the perversion of the natural order, the harm inflicted on the innocent, and the rampant spread of violence and destruction.

5. Uriel, the flame of God, spoke next. He mourned the spiritual corruption of mankind, their hearts led astray by the teachings of the fallen angels.

6. Raphael, the healer of God, expressed sorrow over the physical and spiritual sickness plaguing the world. He grieved for the Earth, scarred and desecrated, and for the humans, whose bodies and souls bore the wounds of their transgressions.

7. Lastly, Gabriel, the strength of God, voiced his outrage over the fallen angels' defiance of God's order. He condemned their lust for power, their arrogance in thinking they could usurp God's authority, and their heartlessness in subjecting mankind to their perverse desires.

8. United in their grief and indignation, the four Archangels made a solemn vow. They would not stand by while the world crumbled. They would appeal to the Most High, the Lord of Creation, to bring justice and restore order.

9. And so, they ascended to the throne of God, their voices ringing out in unison as they appealed for His divine intervention. They prayed for the imprisonment of the fallen angels, the end of the Nephilim, and the cleansing of the Earth.

10. Their words were filled with passion and urgency, their plea echoing through the heavens. They invoked the Lord's mercy for the innocents who suffered and His wrath for the guilty who had caused such suffering.

11. They knew the appeal would have grave consequences. But for the sake of the world, for the preservation of God's creation, they were willing to bear whatever cost their plea might entail.

Chapter XXIII:
Michael, Uriel, Raphael, and Gabriel Appeal to God

1. The Archangels, in their righteous grief and despair, gathered in the celestial realms, their hearts heavy with the burden of the Earth's suffering.

2. Michael, the leader among them, spoke with a voice like thunder, his words echoing with divine authority. "We cannot stand by as the Watchers corrupt God's creation. We must appeal to the Most High."

3. Uriel, the illuminator of truth, agreed with Michael. His voice, steady and resolute, resounded in the ethereal expanse. "The fallen ones have led mankind into darkness. We must call upon the Holy One to guide them back to the path of righteousness."

4. Raphael, the divine healer, nodded solemnly. He spoke softly, yet his words carried the weight of his profound sorrow. "The Earth weeps under the strain of their transgressions. It is our duty to heal what has been broken."

5. Gabriel, the messenger of God, affirmed their shared conviction. His voice, clear and vibrant, rang out with an irrefutable truth. "It is time for us to act. We must stand for justice, for the Earth, and for the children of men."

6. So, they took their pleas to the throne of the Almighty, their words carried on the winds of the heavenly realm, resounding with their shared grief, compassion, and resolve.

7. Michael spoke first, recounting the deeds of the Watchers, their defiance of divine law, and the ruin they had wrought upon the Earth.

8. Uriel, with his discerning gaze, laid bare the depth of mankind's corruption, the darkness that had seeped into their hearts, led astray by the forbidden knowledge imparted by the fallen angels.

9. Raphael, in his merciful nature, pleaded for the healing of the Earth. He shared the cries of the Earth, its rivers tainted, forests burned, and creatures suffering.

10. Gabriel, the herald of divine decrees, demanded justice. He called for the fallen angels to be bound, for their monstrous offspring to be destroyed, and for mankind to be spared from further suffering.

11. Their appeals were impassioned, their voices echoing through the celestial realm. Together, they implored the Most High to intervene, to restore order, and to bring about justice for the fallen world.

Chapter XXIV:
Uriel's Mission to Warn Noah of the Coming Cataclysm

1. Upon hearing the pleas of the archangels, the Most High spoke, His voice resonating throughout the heavens like the gentle hum of creation itself, "Uriel, my illuminator of truth, go forth unto the Earth."

2. "Descend to the son of Lamech, to Noah, the righteous among men. He, who walks in the ways of peace and justice, has found favor in my sight," the Divine Voice continued, filling the celestial realm with its profound authority.

3. Uriel, accepting the divine command, bowed his head in reverence, his countenance reflecting a solemn dedication. "I shall fulfill Your command, O Lord, and warn Noah of the impending doom."

4. Swiftly, Uriel descended from the heavens, his divine form shrouded in a cloak of shimmering starlight, his flight swift as the falling star, brilliant as the morning sun.

5. He found Noah in prayer, his spirit seeking solace in the divine. Uriel approached him, his presence casting a soft, ethereal glow upon the humble surroundings.

6. "Noah," Uriel began, his voice like the rustling of autumn leaves, "I come as a messenger of the Most High, bearing tidings of grave importance."

7. Noah, struck by the celestial visitor, listened intently, his heart beating in tune with the rhythm of divine truth echoing in Uriel's words.

8. "The sins of the fallen angels have tainted the Earth, their monstrous offspring causing chaos and destruction. The Divine Judge has decreed a cleansing—a deluge that will wash away the corruption, leaving only the pure to begin anew."

9. "You, Noah, have been chosen. Build an ark, a vessel to preserve the innocent creatures of the Earth and your righteous family. Through you, life will endure."

10. As Uriel relayed the divine instructions, Noah listened, his spirit awash with a mixture of dread and hope. He understood the gravity of his task, and with a nod, accepted his divine mandate.

11. Uriel, having delivered the divine message, rose to the heavens, leaving Noah with the divine task of preparing for the world's salvation. And thus, the first steps towards the Great Deluge were set into motion.

Chapter XXV:
Punishment of the Fallen Angels

1. In the hallowed halls of Heaven, the voice of the Most High resonated, a solemn decree echoing throughout the celestial realm, "It is time for justice to be served."

2. Turning to Raphael, the Healer of God, the Divine Voice commanded, "Go forth, Raphael, and bind Azâzêl."

3. "Take him, hand and foot, and cast him into the darkness. Make an opening in the desert, which is in Dûdâêl, my divine crucible, and cast him therein."

4. "Upon him place rough and jagged rocks, cover him with darkness, let him abide there for eternity, never to see the light."

5. Raphael, the divine executor of God's justice, bowed, his countenance reflecting steadfast obedience. "Your will be done," he voiced before descending from the heavenly realm.

6. Meanwhile, the Almighty spoke again, this time to Gabriel, the Strength of God, "Proceed against the biters, the reprobates, and the children of fornication. Destroy the children of the Watchers from amongst men."

7. "Send them one against the other, that they may destroy each other in battle. Let the Earth be purged of their wickedness."

8. Gabriel, the warrior of Heaven, unsheathed his sword of divine fire, a symbol of his resolve. With a nod of assent, he prepared for the divine mission.

9. Lastly, to Michael, the Great Prince, the Almighty decreed, "Go, bind Semjâzâ and his associates who have united themselves with women, defiling themselves in their uncleanness."

10. "Bind them fast for seventy generations in the valleys of the Earth, until the day of their judgement and consummation."

11. Michael, the archangel of righteousness and mercy, accepted the divine command with a solemn vow, "Your justice shall be served, O Lord."

12. And so, the archangels descended, each on their divine mission, to execute justice on the fallen angels, to restore order to the Earth, and to prepare for the great cleansing that was to come.

Chapter XXVI:
Raphael Binds Azâzêl

1. Raphael, the divine healer, the embodiment of God's mercy, set forth on his mission, his countenance filled with solemn determination.

2. He descended from the heavens like a falling star, streaking across the sky and landing on Earth with a thunderous echo that resounded through the mountains and valleys.

3. Approaching Azâzêl, Raphael's celestial radiance dimmed the glow of the fallen angel's aura. Azâzêl, once a luminary of Heaven, now stood before Raphael, his features twisted by defiance and bitterness.

4. Unyielding and stern, Raphael declared, "Azâzêl, your transgressions against the divine order have reached the heavens. The Lord has decreed your punishment."

5. With a swift motion, Raphael bound Azâzêl hand and foot. His movements were fluid and precise, each action imbued with divine authority.

6. Azâzêl, once powerful and revered, could offer no resistance. He was powerless against the might of Raphael, the divine agent of God's justice.

7. Raphael cast Azâzêl into the darkness, deep into the desert of Dûdâêl, the divine crucible. There, Azâzêl was to be isolated, hidden from the world he had helped corrupt.

8. The divine healer then placed rough and jagged rocks upon Azâzêl, a physical embodiment of the harsh judgment bestowed upon him.

9. Raphael covered Azâzêl with darkness, blocking all light and hope from reaching him. The once radiant angel was now shrouded in the shadows of his sins.

10. "Here, you shall abide for eternity," Raphael decreed, his voice echoing in the barren expanse of Dûdâêl. "Your light shall never again touch the Earth."

11. With his divine task fulfilled, Raphael ascended back to the heavens, leaving Azâzêl bound and alone, a beacon of God's justice and the consequences of defiance against the divine order.

Chapter XXVII:
Imprisonment in Darkness

1. Once bound, Raphael led Azâzêl to the entrance of a cavernous expanse, the mouth of which seemed to swallow the light of the surrounding desert. This was Dûdâêl, a desolate place set aside by the divine for the punishment of the fallen.

2. Guiding Azâzêl into the abyss, Raphael's divine light became the only source of illumination, casting long, dancing shadows on the uneven walls of the cave.

3. Raphael spoke, his voice echoing in the vast emptiness, "Here in the darkness you will stay, Azâzêl, far from the light of Heaven and Earth."

4. With those words, Raphael cast Azâzêl into the heart of the cave. The fallen angel's cries echoed back, soon swallowed by the stifling darkness.

5. Raphael then began to pile jagged rocks at the mouth of the cave, each stone a testament to Azâzêl's transgressions. The task was laborious, but Raphael, driven by divine duty, did not falter.

6. With the last stone in place, the light within the cave was fully extinguished, plunging Azâzêl into complete darkness. The entrance to Dûdâêl was sealed, and Azâzêl's prison was complete.

7. Raphael stood before the sealed cave, his task completed. "May the weight of your sins press upon you as these stones," he declared. "And may you reflect on your deeds in the lightless void."

8. With that, Raphael departed, leaving Azâzêl alone in the darkness, a prisoner of his own making. The silence of the desert swallowed

his screams, the only testament to his existence the sealed entrance of the cave.

Chapter XXVIII:
Final Judgment in the Fire

1. The divine edict echoed in Raphael's voice, resounding across the vast desert and into the sealed heart of the cave, "Azâzêl, you are bound here until the day of the great judgment."

2. In the silence following his words, the air itself seemed to hold its breath. The finality of this decree was absolute, as unyielding as the stones sealing Azâzêl's fate.

3. "On that day," Raphael continued, his voice stern, echoing with divine wrath, "you shall be cast into the fire, the purifying flames of divine retribution."

4. The promise of this future torment hung in the air, a grim prophecy that would echo in the hollows of Dûdâêl, a constant reminder to Azâzêl of his impending doom.

5. Raphael's gaze lingered on the sealed entrance, his words still hanging in the air. "Your corruption will be cleansed, your sins burned away. Only then will your punishment be complete."

6. The final judgment awaited Azâzêl. He would languish in the darkness, bound and isolated, until the day the divine flames would consume him. The fire would be his end, the final act of divine justice for his sins.

7. Raphael's final words, a divine decree of judgment and punishment, echoed across the desert. As the echoes died, a grim silence fell, a testament to the weight of the divine judgment that had been passed. The fate of Azâzêl was sealed, his end foretold in the consuming fire of divine justice.

Chapter XXIX:
Gabriel's Instructions Regarding the Nephilim

1. Following the judgment of Azâzêl, the Lord turned his attention to the Nephilim, the monstrous offspring of the Watchers and human women. He beckoned Gabriel, His loyal servant, and spoke in a voice that resonated with divine authority.

2. "Gabriel," He began, "You are tasked with a mission of grave importance. You must proceed against the biters and the reprobates, the children born of the unholy union."

3. The term 'biters' referred to the Nephilim who, in their insatiable hunger, consumed all in their path. 'Reprobates' were those who, born of sin, remained unrepentant and uncorrected.

4. The Lord continued, "Destroy the children of fornication, the offspring of the Watchers and mortal women. They are an abomination, a blight upon the face of the Earth."

5. His voice carried a weight that echoed in the silence. "Send them one against the other, let them destroy each other in battle. The blood of their fathers flows within them, they will not hesitate to turn upon one another."

6. Gabriel listened attentively, his countenance stoic as he absorbed the gravity of the task. The eradication of the Nephilim was a divine mandate, a necessary act to restore the balance disrupted by the Watchers.

7. The divine directive given to Gabriel also served as a grim prophecy. The Nephilim, born of the union between celestial beings and humans, were destined for a tragic end – to perish in fratricidal conflict, a reflection of the sins of their fathers.

Chapter XXX:
Destruction of the Nephilim

1. Following the command of the Lord, Gabriel, resolute and unflinching, made his way towards the Earth, his heart burdened by the task ahead.

2. He gazed upon the Nephilim, beings of immense stature and strength, born from the forbidden union of Watchers and humans. Their existence was a violation of the natural order, a testament to the transgressions of their angelic fathers.

3. Gabriel, clothed in divine authority, initiated his divine duty. He instilled confusion and discord among the Nephilim, turning brothers against brothers, friends against friends.

4. The Nephilim, already consumed by their insatiable desires and innate violence, easily fell into the trap laid by Gabriel. Brother fought against brother, friend against friend, their anger and might turning the Earth into a battlefield.

5. The Earth shook under their monstrous might. Mountains crumbled, seas roiled, and the skies thundered with their roars of fury and pain. It was a cataclysm born of heavenly interference and earthly transgression.

6. As the Nephilim battled, their numbers dwindled. Once mighty and feared, they fell, one by one, under the might of their own kin. Their cries echoed across the barren landscapes, a chilling testament to their tragic fate.

7. Thus, the Nephilim, children of the Watchers and human women, met their end. They perished not by the hand of man or angel, but by their own, a result of their monstrous nature and the divine justice enacted upon them.

8. The Earth, once tormented by their presence, slowly began to heal. It was a painful process, a testament to the devastation they had wrought. Yet, the end of the Nephilim marked the beginning of a new era, an era of recovery and rebirth.

9. Meanwhile, Gabriel, having fulfilled his divine mandate, returned to the heavens. His heart was heavy with the knowledge of the destruction he had initiated, yet he knew it was necessary for the preservation of the divine order.

10. Hence, the tragic fate of the Nephilim served as a stark reminder to all creation. It was a testament to the consequences of violating the natural order, of indulging in forbidden unions, and of the inevitable divine justice that follows such transgressions.

Chapter XXXI:
Imprisonment of the Fallen Angels

1. Having witnessed the destruction of the Nephilim, the Lord commanded Michael, the chief of angels, to punish the Watchers, the fathers of the Nephilim. His voice echoed through the heavens, filled with righteous fury and divine judgement.

2. Michael, the mighty warrior angel, prepared for the daunting task. His heart was filled with sorrow for his fallen brethren, yet he was resolved to carry out God's command. For he knew that the order of Heaven and Earth must be preserved, and those who disrupt it must face their due consequences.

3. He descended to Earth, his radiant form lighting up the darkness. He found the fallen angels, once his brothers, now corrupt and pitiful in their fallen state.

4. With divine authority, he bound Semjâzâ, their leader, and his associates. He used chains of light, unbreakable and eternal, crafted by the very hand of God. Their cries of protest were drowned by the howling winds, their pleas for mercy falling on deaf ears.

5. "For seventy generations, you shall be bound in the valleys of the Earth," Michael pronounced, his voice thundering across the barren lands. "You shall witness the passing of time, the rise and fall of generations, yet you shall not partake in them."

6. The fallen angels were left in their earthly prison, their powers restrained, their freedom taken. Their cries echoed through the valleys, a haunting reminder of their fall from grace.

7. "On the day of the great judgement, you shall be led to the abyss of fire," Michael continued, his voice resounding with divine

judgement. "There, you shall face your final doom, an eternal torment for your transgressions."

8. With the fallen angels imprisoned, Michael returned to Heaven. The weight of the task he had just completed weighed heavily on his heart. Yet, he found solace in the knowledge that he had carried out God's command, maintaining the divine order.

9. The fate of the fallen angels served as a stark reminder to all of Heaven and Earth. It was a testament to the consequences of defying God's order, a chilling warning to all who might be tempted to follow in their steps.

10. Thus, the Earth was rid of the fallen angels and their monstrous offspring. However, the scars of their transgressions remained, a painful reminder of a dark time in the history of creation.

Chapter XXXII:
Michael Binds Semjâzâ and Associates

1. The Lord's command to Michael was clear and firm. His voice echoed through the celestial realms, setting the Archangel's task. "Go, bind Semjâzâ and his associates who have united themselves with women and defiled themselves with them in all their uncleanness," he instructed.

2. Michael, the steadfast servant of the Lord, accepted this heavy burden. The thought of binding his brethren was painful, yet he knew he must obey the divine decree. With a heavy heart, he prepared for his journey to Earth.

3. He descended upon the Earth with the authority of Heaven behind him. His divine radiance illuminated the world, casting long shadows behind the fallen ones.

4. He found Semjâzâ, the leader of the fallen angels, and his associates in their earthly abodes. Their once glorious forms were marred by their sinful acts, their divine light dimmed by their transgressions.

5. With a voice that echoed the divine judgment of God, Michael addressed Semjâzâ and his associates. "You have defied the divine order, united yourselves with humans, and brought forth abominations upon this Earth. Now, you must face the consequences of your actions."

6. He bound them with chains of divine light, crafted from the very essence of the divine order they had defied. The chains were unbreakable, their glow unyielding, symbolizing the eternal and unalterable judgement of God.

7. Semjâzâ and his associates struggled against their bindings, their cries of protest and pleas for mercy echoing through the valleys. Yet, the chains held firm, their strength a testament to the unyielding justice of God.

8. Michael, with a heavy heart, completed his task. He left Semjâzâ and his associates bound on Earth, their divine power restrained, their freedom lost. As he ascended back to the heavens, their cries of despair followed him, a painful reminder of their fall from grace.

9. Thus, the fallen angels were bound, their reign of chaos on Earth halted. Their punishment served as a dire warning to all who dared to defy the divine order, a reminder of the price of disobedience to God's law.

10. Michael returned to the heavens, his task complete. Yet, the sorrow of what had transpired lingered, a bittersweet testament to the justice and order of the divine.

Chapter XXXIII:
Imprisonment for Seventy Generations

1. The decree of the Lord, carried out by Michael, was harsh yet just. The fallen angels, led by Semjâzâ, were not only bound but were to be imprisoned for seventy generations.

2. This decree echoed throughout the heavens and the earth, a solemn reminder of the weight of their transgressions. Their punishment was to be long and weary, a test of endurance and a consequence of their defiance.

3. The prison for these fallen ones was the dark and desolate void, a place devoid of light, warmth, and divine presence. There, they were to dwell, bound and isolated from the divine realm they had once called home.

4. Seventy generations of mankind, a span incomprehensible to human understanding, was the duration of their sentence. An era would come and pass, civilizations would rise and fall, and still, their punishment would persist.

5. This lengthy imprisonment was not merely punitive but also served as a deterrent, a cautionary tale for all divine beings. The consequences of defying the divine order and interfering with the affairs of humanity were severe and long-lasting.

6. As the first generation of their sentence commenced, the cries of the fallen angels echoed in the desolate void, their voices filled with regret and despair. Their once divine essence was marred by their actions, and now, they were to face the long and weary consequences.

7. Yet, in their despair, there was a glimmer of divine justice. Their punishment was a testament to the divine order, a stark reminder of the power and authority of the Lord.

8. Thus, for seventy generations, Semjâzâ and his associates would remain, bound and isolated. Their tale of fall and punishment would echo through the ages, a lasting reminder of the divine order and the severe consequences of its defiance.

9. As each generation passed, their story would become a part of the cosmic fabric, a cautionary tale woven into the very essence of creation. Their punishment would serve as a timeless reminder, forever echoing the justice and order of the divine.

10. In the end, their imprisonment for seventy generations was a stern message to all, celestial and terrestrial alike - that defiance of the divine order would not go unpunished, that the justice of the Lord was unyielding and eternal.

Chapter XXXIV:
Confinement in the Abyss of Fire

1. The sentence of the celestial renegades was not solely confined to time, but also to space, a place of torment that matched their transgressions. The fallen angels, led by Semjâzâ, were consigned to the abyss of fire.

2. This abyss, a realm of everlasting flames, was the chosen prison for these fallen ones. It was a place where divine radiance was replaced by destructive fire, where serenity was supplanted by ceaseless torment.

3. The flames of this abyss were not like earthly fire. They were not fueled by wood or stoked by wind, but by the divine justice of the Lord. Each flame danced as a testament to the holy wrath against defiance and disobedience.

4. Here, in this pit of desolation, the fallen angels were to be confined. The scorching flames, a constant reminder of their transgressions, the heat, a symbol of divine anger and disappointment.

5. Bound and chained, they were thrown into this abyss, their divine essence now enveloped by the searing heat of the flames. Their cries of despair drowned by the roar of the inferno that was to be their eternal home.

6. This abyss was not just a prison, but a purgatory. Every flame, every ember, served to purge their beings of the corruption they had embraced. Yet, the cleansing was eternal, for their sins were of such magnitude that they could never be fully purged.

7. As each generation passed, the flames of the abyss never abated. They continued to burn, fueled by the divine justice, their heat a stark reminder of the wrath of the Lord.

8. The confinement in the abyss of fire was a testament to the divine order. It echoed the consequences of rebellion, the cost of meddling in the affairs of mankind, and the punishment for defying the Lord.

9. Through this punishment, the Lord proclaimed his divine authority. No angel, no matter how divine, could defy his will and disrupt the harmony of creation without facing severe repercussions.

10. Thus, for seventy generations, Semjâzâ and his associates were to dwell in the abyss of fire. Their screams of torment echoed throughout the cosmos, a grim reminder of the price of defiance and disobedience to the divine order.

Chapter XXXV:
The Judgment and Consummation of the Fallen Angels

1. The time of reckoning approached for the fallen angels, led astray by their own vanity and curiosity. The Heavenly Court was convened, the divine judgment was prepared.

2. In the presence of the Most High, the angels who had defied the divine order were brought forward. Their once radiant faces now marred by the torment of the abyss, their once mighty wings now charred and useless.

3. The Lord, in His infinite wisdom and justice, pronounced His final judgment upon the fallen. They were to face the ultimate consequence of their rebellion - their consummation.

4. This was not a mere destruction, but a complete erasure of their existence. Their divine essence was to be stripped away, their memories and deeds wiped from the annals of time.

5. The heavenly host watched in solemn silence as the sentence was passed. The once revered leaders of angelic hosts, now pariahs, were to face the unthinkable - the end of their eternal existence.

6. The fallen angels, in their despair, pleaded for mercy. They spoke of repentance, of their desire for redemption. But the Lord, in His wisdom, knew their hearts. Their pleas were empty, their repentance insincere.

7. The Lord reminded them of their transgressions, of the chaos they had brought upon the Earth. They had been entrusted with the stewardship of creation, yet they had forsaken their duty, succumbing to their own desires.

8. The execution of the judgment was swift. One by one, the fallen angels were consumed. Their cries of despair faded into nothingness, their presence extinguished from the universe.

9. As each fallen angel was consumed, a wave of divine energy swept through the heavens. It was a stark reminder of the divine order, the consequences of defiance, and the absolute authority of the Lord.

10. And so, the fallen angels were no more. Their tales of rebellion became a solemn warning to the heavenly host. The divine order was restored, and peace once again reigned in the heavens. The Earth, too, began to heal from the havoc wrought by the fallen, preparing itself for a new era of righteousness under the watchful eye of the faithful angels.

Chapter XXXVI:
The Eternal Binding of the Condemned

1. After the divine judgment was executed, the heavenly court turned to the matter of the eternal binding of the condemned. The Lord, in His infinite wisdom, knew that their transgressions had to be forever sealed, an eternal testament to the dire consequences of rebellion against the divine order.

2. Michael, the archangel of justice, was called forth. With a stern expression, he held the divine chains in his hands, each link forged from the divine will itself. These were not ordinary chains; they were designed to bind the essence of the condemned, ensuring their eternal imprisonment.

3. The chains shimmered with divine energy, pulsating with the force of righteousness. Michael, bearing the heavy weight of this task, began the process of binding. One by one, the remnants of the fallen angels were chained, their essence forever bound within the confines of the divine chains.

4. Each chain was imbued with a divine seal, an eternal mark that symbolized the fallen angel's transgressions. The seals were unique, reflecting the specific acts of rebellion committed by each fallen angel.

5. As the binding took place, the heavens were filled with a solemn silence. Each divine seal marked the end of a tale of rebellion and the beginning of an eternity of confinement. The divine chains were then cast into the abyss, where the essence of the fallen would remain, bound and isolated.

6. Michael, the archangel of justice, performed his duty with unwavering resolve. Each chain was cast with a stern prayer, a plea

for the universe to remember the consequences of rebellion, the price of defying the divine order.

7. With the final chain cast into the abyss, the task of eternal binding was complete. Michael stood before the Lord, his duty fulfilled. The heavenly court observed in solemn silence, the weight of the moment not lost on them.

8. The Lord, in His infinite wisdom, spoke. His words echoed throughout the heavens, a final testament to the fallen. "Let their tales be a reminder," He said, "of the consequences of rebellion. Let their eternal binding serve as a warning to all who dare defy the divine order."

9. And thus, the final chapter of the fallen angels was written. Their tales of rebellion were forever sealed, their existence confined to the abyss. The heavenly host returned to their duties, their hearts filled with a renewed sense of purpose and a solemn reminder of the price of rebellion.

10. The Earth, too, began its process of healing. The havoc wrought by the fallen was gradually erased, and a new era of peace began. The faithful angels watched over the Earth, guiding and protecting humanity as they had been entrusted to do. The tale of the fallen served as a constant reminder of their duty, of the importance of maintaining the divine order.

11. In the end, the eternal binding of the condemned served not just as a punishment, but also as a lesson. It was a clear message to all creation - the divine order is sacred, and defiance comes with a heavy price. The tale of the fallen angels, their rebellion, and their eternal binding became an integral part of the cosmic lore, a story retold throughout the ages, a lesson for all beings in the universe.

www.ingramcontent.com/pod-product-compliance
Lightning Source LLC
Chambersburg PA
CBHW032134090426
42743CB00007B/593